Mirror of the Orient

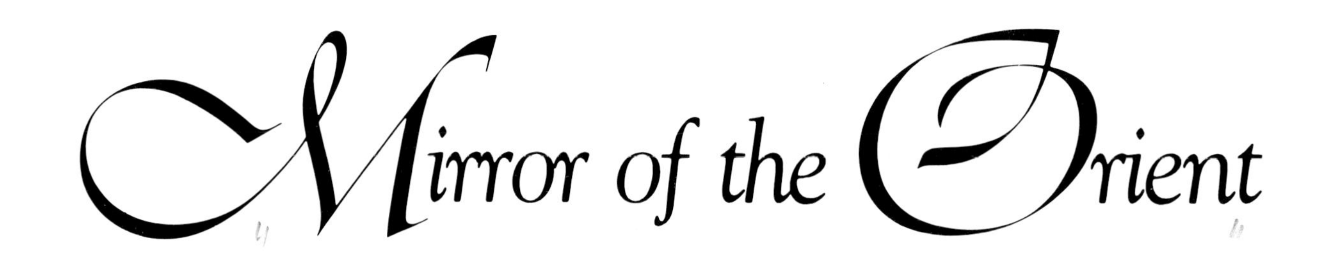

Mirror of the Orient

ROLAND AND SABRINA MICHAUD

Foreword by Najm ud-Din Bammat

NEW YORK GRAPHIC SOCIETY • *Boston*

For Jean-Claude Michaud

Text translated from the French by Robert Vollrath

International Standard Book Number:
0-8212-1129-3
Library of Congress Catalog Card Number:
81-81624

First published in France by Hachette Réalités
First English language edition

Printed in Switzerland

New York Graphic Society books are published by Little, Brown and Company. Published simultaneously in Canada by Little, Brown and Company (Canada) Limited.

To begin with, two stories: one solemn, the other frivolous. They reflect mutually, each in the other; like the play of light from two mirrors, they are two refracted images.

First, the meeting between Averroës and Ibn Arabi, according to tradition. The former is the master of physical science. The latter, still young when the visit takes place, will become the master of metaphysical knowledge.

Averroës was the physician; it was he, for Europe, who founded rationalism and who "composed the commentary of Aristotle" — "colui che il gran Commentario feo," as Dante will write. Moukh ud-Din Ibn Arabi was, for the Orient, the mystic, "sheikh al akbar," the greatest of the sheikhs, the spiritual initiator.

With this rigorous confrontation between two truths, the real value of existence would be revealed. Averroës — admired, famous, and craftsman of a remarkable work — is curious to sound out the wisdom of young Ibn Arabi. Word of his intuitive vision had been spreading. Averroës thus rises upon seeing the young Ibn Arabi, who enters. Ibn Arabi can sense the generosity of Averroës, who warmly greets him with open arms and who extends to him the wealth of his thought and the fruits of his science. He offers none other than the vast stores of positivity painstakingly acquired through a life of rigorous reflection, methodically conducted upon the basis of concrete experimentation with reality. To all this, Ibn Arabi responds, "Yes." Averroës breaks into a broad smile.

Then Ibn Arabi responds, again with one single word: "No." Analytically verifiable science, demanding of the facts it observes, plying its strategies, consuming tangible experience, is very possibly efficient and useful. To this science, yes. But it ensnares itself without understanding any other end than itself, and would presume its own authority as the ultimate discourse. In this case, it can only close itself off, confined to its own interior, imprisoned in its own positivity.

In the too rapid expression of joy Averroës exhibited, a certain complacency is revealed: intellectual comfort, with the hollow certitude of knowledge fat and satisfied with itself. Thus: "No."

Averroës' comment, again as tradition would have it: "Within the space of this 'yes' and this 'no,' my demise is lodged; and heads are wrenched from the neck, and souls from the body." "Wrenched from the neck," a brutal image for disarticulation quickly followed by a rupture. The mind is hurled into a vacuum, and this abrupt rift in the very night of reason eliminates all points of reference, all security.

The second story concerns a banquet. There were in Baghdad two vizirs in the caliph's service. It was unclear which of the pair was the more refined, so superlative was the taste and splendor of each. The caliph's court urged him to put them to the test: he consented, and decided as the criterion that each should arrange a banquet. He who organized the most elegant display would be the ultimate authority on taste and etiquette. Thus the day arrived for the first of the competitors. Upon entering the banquet hall, what was to be found? Perfection itself. All without flaw: the guest selection, the quality of the menu, the embellishment of the hall uniting fresh elegance with brilliant lighting, all lacking any obvious artifice. There were poems recited, music and dance, edifying but friendly conversation, at times erudite, but always witty. All was truly perfect; to imagine a better presentation was impossible. The other contestant seemed doomed. Some already mourned his defeat. Others, more enterprising, commenced paying their court to the obvious victor.

One week later, the night of the second banquet arrived. There was at first extreme curiosity, then great surprise, finally a profound disappointment. Surprise and disappointment arose because of the nature of this second banquet: it was in every way, point by point, identical to the previous one. The same guests were invited, the hall's arrangement and decoration a repetition. Identical were the poems, the melodies and dancing. There were the same flowers and the same fragrances. Conversation took up again as a repetition of itself. Echoes and reflections. It was impossible for the frustrated guests to criticize the plagiarist; holding their tongues, they began to enjoy themselves.

After a short while, the caliph announced, "Today's banquet has won. May the Lord's benediction follow its maker always, just as will our delighted appreciation for the exceptional moment he has given us, and which we shall forevermore savor in our memories."

The stunned hall showed no reaction. What if the caliph spoke ironically? This supposition seemed likely, and, in fact, was the only possible explanation.

Finally, the great vizir came forth, urged on by the crowd, and dared ask, "Oh great and illustrious caliph! In your unsparing justness, you perhaps wanted to laugh at the impertinence of this unlucky one, or else, in your boundless wisdom, you have seen what our eyes were not capable of seeing. If your limitless indulgence would accept to clear up this matter for us, please share the reasons for your choice."

And the caliph responded, "I do not know what to say, in truth, because the reason is subtle and avoids clear explanation.

"We had almost forgotten that moment we lived but a week ago. Now, this vizir's art has restored through a dreamlike repetition all the magic that had disappeared, all the evaporated perfume from the shattered flask. What occurred the other night simply occurred. But the reflection we saw this evening was a true act of creation: this reflection has tapped and actually restored our flow of happiness in its spontaneous perfection. In addition, it gave us three other treasures: memory, recognition, and victory over the annihilation of the past. No success is sweeter than this!"

In more modern terms, the caliph announced that the first banquet was simply a natural fact; the second was fully and consciously a cultural phenomenon. "Verweile doch, du bist so schön" — stop, wait — or again, "endure, linger, for you are so beautiful," Goethe's Faust will say at the moment of accomplished perfection, before consenting to die. Goethe was among the first Europeans to love the Orient. Western and modern he remained, however, because the instant of which he speaks concerns not a feast, but a task. And the *West-östlicher Divan* neglects so many things! The repetition that enchants the caliph recaptures the fortuitous event. Through the force of style, which recreates, and memory, which recalls, that event is given eternal value. In so doing, it also preserves its freshness, fragránce, and taste. Herein lies true art.

These two tales concern the juxtaposition of two realities mirrored: both in the dialogue between the two masters as with the two banquets in Baghdad. Here, as there, it is the refraction of the "nearly similar," the slight slippage from the similar to the same, which creates and brings forth inner truth.

Captured by Roland and Sabrina Michaud, the pictures contained in this book reveal, through a play of mirrors, a reality that confronts itself. The past and present gaze at each other: permanent truths of Muslim civilization emerge. Faced with this confrontation, the viewer should especially beware any nostalgia for the past, anachronistic folklore or resigned stagnation. Here, these facile clichés have never been more inappropriate. Such judgments have often been applied to those who sincerely love Islam, as, in fact, to Islam itself. At bottom, however, the movements and gestures presented here are not anachronistic, but outside time, ordinary and yet forever vibrant. These photographs must not be seen simply as beautiful, noble, or humble (although they are most often all three at once); they rather recall, through their reflection, a permanence. In turn, this permanence is not the sign of stiffness due to decline and old age, but reveals a source of life and fidelity which, in the people, guarantees Islamic cultural identity.

Actually, the division does not come between the so-called traditional cultures and those which are modern. The true distinction concerns the separation between authentic cultures — lived, loved, those which give meaning to life, essentially fulfilled and without "class" distinctions — and artificial or borrowed cultures. People of these latter wear culture as a coat, from the outside; they are stereotypes of escapism, even if they do benefit from an enormous "mass media."

Sabrina and Roland Michaud have looked at the Orient with lively and life-giving eyes. They have loved it for itself, in its essence and beyond all trends of fashion. It was, incidentally, their passion for Afghanistan which put me in contact with them. They have imported the most beautiful images of it.

I am reminded how, in certain areas, marriage engagement festivities open with the waiting at the mirror. I am not sure if the custom exists elsewhere in the world of Islam, but I imagine that it does.

See her enter, the promised fiancée. Having never yet been seen, she appears for the first time. She advances, emerging from the distance and moves from the background, outside the field of vision, into the immediate, almost tactile, presence of the mirror. Emergence from darkness into light. Her discovery is thus indirect, by refraction. It is also intimate, the very closeness of a prolonged gaze into this mirror, placed just in front of the viewer. The surface may even be slightly steamed up from his breath as he waits. Through this cloudy surface, in these quivering reflections projected by the dancing candlelight, the emerging image becomes confused with his waiting face. There is a fusion of reflections. Meanwhile, the reflection that unites them also throws them back, blurred, into another space, but which is also their innermost being: refraction upon refraction, light upon light. Thus the great play of one and of two is already beginning. Play of mirrors, but also of civilizations, from one period to another. "The double exile where the double melts into one." Thus spoke Catherine Pozzi. She had resumed the tradition of the former Lyonnaise, Louise Labé. But, in turn, this dialogue echoes, in style and in spirit, blazons and courtly love from the *langue d'oc* and the *dolce stil nuovo,* just as the abundant Arab, Persian, and Turkish languages recall Leyla and Majnun, Yusuf and Zuleika, wild Andalusian love, and yet farther back, the Hedjazians, Yemenites, and, still farther, the great hermetic and Platonic themes, until the very immemorial myths where the distinction between West and East is abolished.

It is thus not surprising that this theme is used in spiritual initiation as well. In certain Sufi orders, the first challenge of the initiation consists in a confrontation — solitary and silent — between the person and his shadow as seen in a mirror. The image is reflected in its identical, or rather, near identity.

Either the imperfections of this ancient mirror or its very depth, giving the smooth surface an opaqueness, returns a slightly pale, fuzzy image: the lines are imperceptibly effaced. While trying to recognize yourself in the captured image, it simultaneously flees and approaches you in its doubling of a repetitive displacement. Yes and no. Between this "yes" and this "no" . . .

A confrontation between the self and the Self, between a fleeing identity, subject to death, and this other identity . . . But how can we indicate the inconceivable? The masters of this, which we have isolated only through a reflection of it, call it respectfully the "Sirr," secret or mystery, to avoid any vain attempt to name it.

"As in a glass darkly," Muslim tradition finds a Christian echo: "He is revealed only in veils of shadow and light. For without this mercy, the world would instantaneously burst into flames confronted with His Face, and, as quickly, fall into ash."

Reality cannot be grasped. It cannot be split apart or reduced down. Any conceptual philosophy is thwarted *a priori.* Only negatively are we permitted any expectation or hope (perhaps also any merit) that the veiling of being and the unveiling of the revelation take place. For mankind, only in the "no" is the "yes" made possible. This sighting through the shadows of a "yes" and "no" is expressed in Muslim art by means of the arabesque.

At first sight, the arabesque is a whimsical play of forms composed of traces of writing, organic motifs, angles and bends. Its splendor seems to be self-sufficient, like life itself. But beyond the lines, which melt and turn over one another, behind the colorful mirroring, close scrutiny reveals a stable geometry. The unfolding forms are actually constructed from simple figures — triangles, pentagons and others — which engender the lines and their folds infinitely. The physical marks seem to give way to abstract rhythm, in turn producing a secret proliferation, appearance and multiplicity. The projected, blended figures, seemingly whimsical in their meanderings, are based on stable relationships.

It is in this major way that "the arabesque is the most ideal of all forms," as Baudelaire will write. Similarly, snow, beyond its soft, melting whiteness, is based on a crystalline structure of strict mathematical regularity, but which can be extended indefinitely.

The tracing of the arabesque is thus the shadow of a reality that transcends all description. By means of a network of lines, it provides the sensory impression of an absolute, like a metaphor for the invisible. An untenable claim, it would seem, but only the art through which Islam is expressed can make it.

Numerous examples of figurative art exist, it is true, but the art of Islam is not naturalistic. For the most part, Muslim art long ago turned away from the parody of creation, describing the exterior appearance of things. Muslim art does not concern itself with an imitative doubling of nature, a sterile repetition; rather it evokes the source of all creation. This evocation of the ungraspable can only be managed through indirect allusion. There is just enough form to animate space: thus the arabesque, the shimmer of glazed faience, the illumination. Just enough sound to make the silence vibrate: thus Oriental music.

The arabesque is therefore both respect for transcendency and a commentary on the infinite unfolding of creation — not as things in creation, but as its very principle as revealed in rhythm and in musical and visual harmonies. Form returns to life, music to sole musicality. Exegesis in theology or in Muslim law, commentary in philosophy, metaphor in literature: all these give witness to the same respect for ultimate reality as the arabesque or monody. Too often exterior analysts have interpreted these aspects of classical Islam as a lack of creative power in the artist, or even as a lack of originality. That completely misses the point.

The point is truth. Respect for that ultimate reality demands that we avoid reproducing the simulacrum, the exterior form, in order to better call up, from the interior — in the very spirit of the viewer, listener or thinker — the spark which allows us to perceive the source of all creation, truth or beauty. This spark, however short-lived, opens up into the absolute. The work of art strikes and flares up, translucence illuminating consciousness. "No construction of concepts," said Jalal ud-Din Rumi, "I want an all-consuming fire." Through arabesque, commentary or metaphor, the decisive imaginative and creative act belongs no longer to an individual author, but to whoever perceives and feels. Thus we understand the uniqueness of the poem: simultaneously an aesthetc, spiritual and moral vision which, in verbal economy, turns the reader toward himself. The place of tales also comes to light: verbally profuse, they abruptly invite one of the listeners to tell another story within the story, on to infinity. This endless setting in the narration tends to abolish the distance between author and listener, all the while multiplying — as in a play of reflections — the tale's shimmer and reverberation.

The thousand and *first* night. The importance of this extra night has been noted by the Lebanese poet Saleh Stetie, whose work holds a major significance, in French as in Arabic. The thousand and first night, in reality neither first nor last, signals the rupture with symmetry — a symmetry mortal in its undifferentiated regularity. This extra night signifies the skip outside of the established, the barely perceptible warp in the reflection which lets there "be something rather than nothing." In this way an asymmetry or imperfection is worked into fine tapestries. As opposed to a naturalistc theater of actors, the various theaters which make use of shadows, puppets and masks also find their reason in this slight irregularity, not only in Islam but everywhere in the Orient. The theater and its double. But in this refraction, which one is the double?

The Catholic Church's ancient mistrust of acting and its hesitation to bury an actor on consecrated ground stem from the same principle as the arabesque and shadow in Muslim art. God must measure souls in their truth. Man must not complicate the rules by pretending to be something he is not. Translated into humanistic terms, the same reticence appears in Montaigne, in his essay about the danger of imitating infirmity and illness. This reluctance can be explained by an ancient fear of suddenly being enslaved by the imitation, captive of the counterfeit. A counterfeit art: I have finally come upon the expression I have been looking for. It describes the naturalistic type of art. It counterfeits, gives depth and thickens contours; that, Islam rejects.

But suspicion of the figure "which produces shadow" reaches far back in history, into the sensibility of the peoples who later transmitted Islam. Even the pre-Islamic Arab poems begin with the discovery of an abandoned camp. After this necessary introduction, the remainder of the poem belongs to memory, digging up the past. The text is in the past tense, or, more precisely, is translated by the future perfect. Right away, the poem is told as a poem, and only as a poem. It is literary re-creation and not pretense to create a world rivaling nature. Here again, it does not simulate; rather, it indicates. This is why the style is so important. It is precisely in this way, through style rather than juxtaposition, that Roland and Sabrina Michaud create the spark which, for a passing instant, lights up the eternal.

There is a continuity in these Central Asian landscapes, where, abruptly, the steppe and the garden meet. Here are the dreams of mankind: aridity and work have nurtured blossoms in the heart of the desert. These two adjacent scenes create a calligraphy, so frequent in these places where the object is inscribed into a background of drought.

There is a calligraphy here, in one of the images, to the point of showing how the written trace is produced with almost the same spirit and movement as the line of a tree. The images remind us that Islam is embedded in the geography of antiquity. Between civilizations assured of their centrality, it established a space of communication. It reached out over a vast common area to permit economic, financial, intellectual, and trade exchanges. Peoples of the Mediterranean and the Middle East, Byzantines and Sassanids, India and China, all were attached to this enormous new space of communication. Outside of the "urbs" and "polis" of the Central Empires, only the barbarians had posed a threat. Now even they were reunited with civilization under Islam's umbrella. Soon the barbarians themselves will found new dynasties and lead empires.

Within this image offered to us, we are reminded that Islam, "median" or "intermediate community" as the Koran itself says, is not only at home in a Mediterranean mixture, but also within the borders of India, Central Asia, and China. And we find yet another pair of images: in this flat, open space of communication, whether desert or steppe, Islam has settled within an archipelago of cities connected by a commerce of caravans. Man settles where he raises his tent. This is an impermanent habitation where movement is always possible; the only stable orientation is fixed by faith, toward Mecca, the only true city grouping all Muslims in an extraterritorial city.

Within this nomadic world, Roland and Sabrina Michaud show us how a horse is captured. Taoist Chinese imagery showed us the proper steps for capturing a cow. Here we see the same rapid prehension, the same force concentrated on the object with the same mindful — or even spiritual — presence. It is a stunning act of vitality, commanded in an instant by consciousness in the very awareness of its concentration. This spiritual presence thus coincides, again through mirrored reflection, with the tumultuous flow of the events themselves.

This recalls certain images of dervishes from then and now, some calm in their silent meditation, others bursting with hilarity, and even breaking into dance. "Malengs," or mad masters, wise beyond sanity and madness — these conceptual pairs being simple appearance — have been photographed to show that the type has not yet died out. I once sent a European to Central Asia to work with a certain master. He confided to him that he no longer knew exactly where he was, somewhere between consciousness and forgetfulness, between his profession and his temptations, between different cultures, as if fighting all sorts of contradictory currents. The answer from the master came in a single word: "Flow." This direct response was one of life, turning this visitor inward toward himself, toward his center, what he had previously been fleeing. Centrifugal. "I fled out of myself toward you, when I heard a voice crying from myself into me," utters the Muslim mystic. Perhaps the most striking picture of this album is the dancer in the snow, simultaneously wise and regally mad; in fact, his spinning is beyond sanity and madness.

Doesn't this ecstatic knowledge overflowing with joy, this presence showing no concern for the snowfall, dusting all, this full "yes" to life, recall someone? Nietzsche, perhaps, and his Dionysus, but especially his Zarathustra. Jubilation in a snowy solitude — dancing knowledge. Zarathustra seized in his homeland. "Vaterländischer Wiederkehr," return to the hearth, and passing through the focal point of the Orient — this is the visual beauty of Roland and Sabrina Michaud.

Face to face, skipping not only centuries but also social conditions: the sultan and the destitute smell the same flower. Here one can dance to the principle of renewal: "the renewal of creation at every instant." Different from the linear flow of time, Islam knows another time, where the instant is pregnant with eternity, where each new minute echoes the noise of creation on its first day. Thus each moment has the glowing vitality of this horse we saw struggling against its fetters or the freshness of this flower. The portrait of the sultan also reveals a meeting between the Orient and the West. Look first at the miniature, then at the photograph. This is what so moved the Bellinis. The style, if not the treatment, remains traditional, especially the gesture. The conqueror is not shown as the soldier spurring his horse. He is a lawmaker; he is not shown as a sovereign. Sitting cross-legged, he gazes at nothing. The picture gives us the simple detour of a passing instant: this fragrance. The pictures of this album fold over on themselves: repetition, confirmation, but also a slight difference into which our own reflection tumbles. The distance here is not one of exoticism. This rediscovery is no longer naive, a simple gesture equal to itself both in the past and in the present. More subtle, this fold is both more intimate and impossible to complete: it separates us from ourselves. It comprises our innermost being.

Here, I am reminded of a Hindu phrase, as if by ricochet, because it comes by way of contemporary Latin American literature. It is from Julio Cortázar. "When two things are perceived with the same consciousness of the interval between them, you must place yourself in that interval. In this way, the two things are eliminated, and Reality will shine forth." That is the sixtieth stanza of the Vijnana Bhairava. It also seems to illustrate what these photographs show, pair by pair.

But let me go on to another confrontation, this time not between two illustrations, but between two living beings. Pilgrims are arriving at the Kaaba at Mecca. Everywhere else, they stand side by side, only an abstract expression on their faces. But at Mecca itself, at the end — or rather at the very center — of their journey, the faithful group around, not linearly but in a circle, toward one axial point. Here in this place, the straight bends, the linear is transformed into a circle. At that moment, the Muslim discovers another face on the side opposite him. On this route, in the absence of any icon, altar, or tabernacle, the last meeting is not with a symbol, but another living, breathing being. Having come from the opposite horizon, but with the same intention, that other being seems to reflect him. There is physical as well as intentional symmetry. Verification could be made by folding the circumference over the central point. As if reversed in a mirror, the community is still one. The circle is complete.

There exists a fraternity in the community, all the more powerful because it passes through a central absolute reference. The other being, opposite, could be rich or poor, strong, able or oppressed. Any and all differences are abolished. "Praise," says the parable, "to Him who erases all names, conditions, professions and qualities to allow simply for being." Everyone is unified even in their appearance, for they wear the *ihram,* the shoulder- and loincloth of a uniform white. All are effaced behind this whiteness, all newborn, all already in the beyond. Similarly, the Koran begins with the Fatiha, a praise of the Unique, and closes with the "surat an-nas," the chapter of humanity. This word "nas," "people," is repeated five times in six measured verses. The Koran closes on itself as if ready for a new reading, just as the pilgrimage to Mecca closes with a new departure.

The uninterrupted reading of the Koran repeats the first verses which overlap the last ones. Thus, man's presence is echoed in the consciousness of Unity, itself then repeated in the human sphere. The community is unified and transcended while the One and Transcendent remains.

But it is in Islam's profession of faith, the Shalada, where this symmetry between the relative and the absolute is most firmly expressed. "La ilaha illa Allah." "Nothing divine if not God." No being if not Being. But, remember, this is not a duality. The two parts of the formula do not indicate a progression of binary opposition. We are as far as possible from dialectics. Exactly that which has been negated, in disjointed and ephemeral form, is affirmed, in unity.

The name which is above all being, "huwa," "Him," when produced in a certain hand is written in a right-to-left symmetry, as if in a mirror.

Similarly, the two parts, negative and positive, of the profession of faith mirror each other in the finite and the infinite. In the middle of the utterance, a rift or caesura is produced by holding one's breath.

Exactly as the rosary contains ninety-nine beads, the hundredth being the very breath of the chanter, the silence, between the "yes" and "no" of the Shalada takes place within the believer's very being. "Within the space of this yes and this no, the neck is wrenched from the shoulders." Within this caesura between the two terms of the profession of faith, in this disclosure of being, this vacuum of any conceivable meaning, the unutterable comes to be inscribed.

Najm ud-Din Bammat

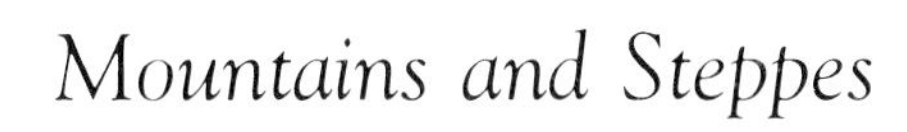

Mountains and Steppes

Hunter with greyhound
Hunter with bow
Falconer
"Tent-pegging"
Horse-breaking
Horsemen

Hunter with greyhound

1 Seventeenth-century Persian miniature. Composite album. State Library, Leningrad, U.S.S.R.

2 November 1964. Chesht, Afghanistan. The greyhound in Afghanistan is treated with special attention. It is reserved exclusively for hunting.

Hunter with bow

3 December 1967. Kamdesh, Nuristan Province, Afghanistan.
The stone bow has a double string joined in the middle with a piece of leather. The stone replaces the arrow of a traditional bow.

4 Miniature from a sixteenth-century manuscript, *Lights of Canopus*. Collection of the Marquess of Bute, England.

Falconer

5 January 1973. Master Jura Eshan and his falcon. Village of Tauz Bulak, Afghan Turkistan.
Game consists of quail, rabbit, fox, and wolf, with which the hunter barters for the food and clothing he needs in order to live within the community.

6 Seventeenth-century Persian miniature. School of Isfahan. The Louvre, Paris.

Overleaf
Miniature from a seventeenth-century atlas in the University of Istanbul Library, Turkey.

May 1967. Hills in the spring, Kunduz Province, Afghanistan.

"Tent-pegging"

7 Detail from a sixteenth-century Turkish miniature, from a *Book of Feasts* by Loqman. Topkapi Museum Library, Turkey.

8 August 1967. Independence Day celebration in Kabul, Afghanistan.
This Pashtun game of skill has a galloping rider pick up a wooden peg protruding no more than eight inches out of the ground. This he must accomplish with a hooked lance.

Horse-breaking

9 February 1973. Training for a Bozkashi tournament in the Andkhui region of Afghan Turkistan.
Rest before the challenge: the horse, relieved of his saddle and harness, circles around under the guidance of a trainer before rolling in the dust, his four hooves in the air.

10 Siyah Kalem miniature, fifteenth century. *Album of the Conqueror.* Topkapi Museum Library.

Horsemen

11 Miniature from a fourteenth-century *Book of Kings.* Faramurz, son of Rustam, pursues the fleeing army of the king of Kabul. The Louvre, Paris.

12 February 1968. Bozkashi tournament on the steppes of Afghan Turkistan, Dowlatabad, Balkh Province, Afghanistan.
The famous Bozkashi is a game of skill on horseback. The Turkish peoples of Central Asia engage in it enthusiastically on Fridays and on festive occasions during the winter.

1

کودکی برسم عادت بر حوالی کشت میگشت چون چشمش بر کبوتر افتاد سوز سودای
کباب دود از دلش بر آورد از روی دست مهره در کمان کرده بپیوست بازمانده از آن بازی
غافل و بجانب کشت زار بطلب و طوف
مرغزار و صحرا مایل که ناگاه از شعبده فلک
حقه باز اثر ضرب آن مهره بر بال آن شکسته

4

6

7

8

11

12

Caravans

Shepherd
Camel-tethering
Camp
Tending the fire
Autumn migration

Shepherd

13 March 1973. Dowlatabad, Meymaneh Province, Afghanistan.
Caracul lambs born prematurely furnish precious Astrakhan furs. Astrakhan is the name of the port located on the Volga from where these furs used to be exported. Indigenous to the Bukhara region, caracul sheep are perfectly adapted to the rough, dry climate of Turkistan.

14 Seventeenth-century Persian miniature by Master Riza Abbasi. Composite album. State Library, Leningrad, U.S.S.R.

Camel-tethering

15 Fifteenth-century miniature. Topkapi Museum Library, Istanbul, Turkey.

16 January 1971. Wakham Corridor, Afghanistan.
After being unloaded in the evening, the camels, protected by a felt covering, are tied head to foot. This position keeps the sweat-covered animals from rolling on the ground and catching cold. After two hours they are released.

Camp

17 Sixteenth-century Persian miniature. *Book of Kings*, Ferdowsi, Museum of Turkish and Islamic Arts, Istanbul, Turkey.

18 January 1971. A camp of Kirghiz tents at twelve thousand feet, Afghan Pamir.
The tents of the Turko-Mongol peoples are made from collapsible willow pieces around which is attached thick felt. Felt efficiently protects against the cold.

Tending the fire

19 Detail from a fifteenth-century Siyah Kalem miniature. *Album of the Conqueror.* Topkapi Museum Library, Istanbul, Turkey.

20 March 1968. Turkman shepherd preparing a plate of rice in a caravanserai in Tashkurgan, Afghanistan.

Autumn migration

21 Miniature from a Nizami manuscript, *Treasure of Secrets.* Ṣchool of Herat, fifteenth century. Museum of Turkish and Islamic Arts, Istanbul, Turkey.

22 September 1970. Kashgai nomads traveling. Fars Province, Iran.

13

14

17

18

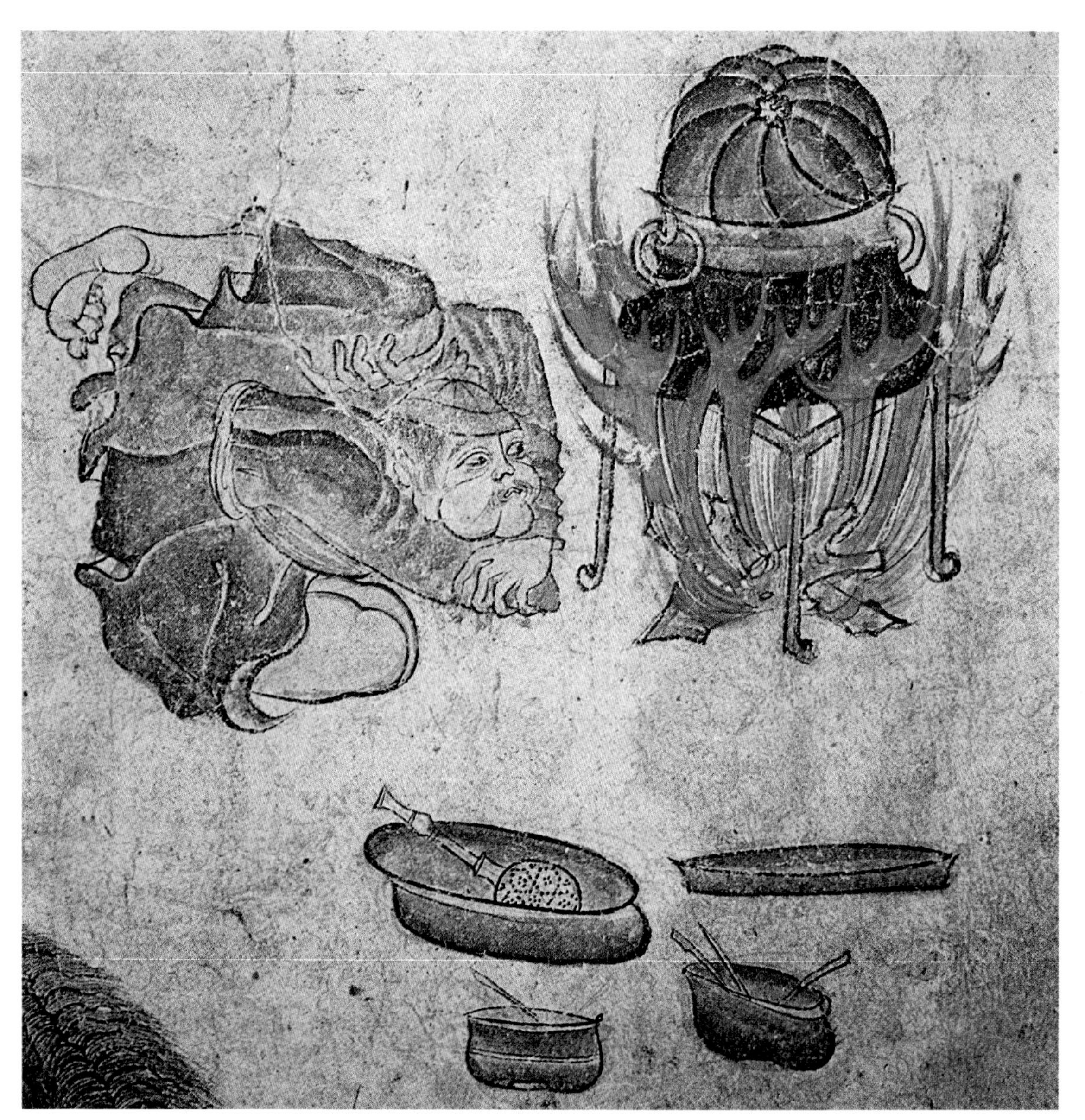

21

22

Bazaars

Exchanges
Weighing
Carding
The distaff and the spinning wheel
The raft
Lake in Kashmir

Exchanges

23 Detail from a miniature by Siyah Kalem, fifteenth century. *Album of the Conqueror.* Topkapi Museum Library, Istanbul, Turkey.

24 March 1968. Mazar-i-Sharif, Afghanistan.

Overleaf
Eighteenth-century Turkish miniature. *Book of Feasts* by Vehbi. Topkapi Museum Library, Istanbul, Turkey.

June 1968. Barber working in the streets, Isfahan, Iran.

Weighing

25 Detail from a Mogul miniature. *Book of Babur,* sixteenth century. National Museum of Delhi, India.

26 May 1967. Weighing scene in a caravanserai at Tashkurgan, Afghanistan.

Carding

27 Miniature from a nineteenth-century Indo-Persian manuscript on occupations and trades in Kashmir. India Office Library, London, England.

28 January 1968. Khost, Paktia Province, Afghanistan.
The tool used is a kind of bow attached to a sheepgut string. Using the string softens the blows of the swingle. This first bow is connected to a second one, which is attached from above. The assembly thus multiplies the vibrations and better cleans the wool.

The distaff and the spinning wheel

29 Eighteenth-century Persian miniature. Composite album. University of Istanbul Library, Turkey.

30 November 1964. Spinner at the wheel in the Herat Prison, Afghanistan.

The raft

31 Sixteenth-century Mogul miniature from the *Book of Babur*. National Museum of Delhi, India.

32 January 1978. Crossing the Konar River, Nangarhar Province, Afghanistan. When there is no bridge, river-crossings are made using simple rafts, assemblages of branches buoyed by goatskins ballooned with air.

Lake in Kashmir

33 Miniature from a nineteenth-century Indo-Persian manuscript on occupations and trades in Kashmir. India Office Library, London, England.

34 July 1978. Boat on Lake Nagin at Srinagar, Indian Kashmir.
The *shikara,* local boats provided with a small straw roof, are steered with wooden, heart-shaped paddles.

29

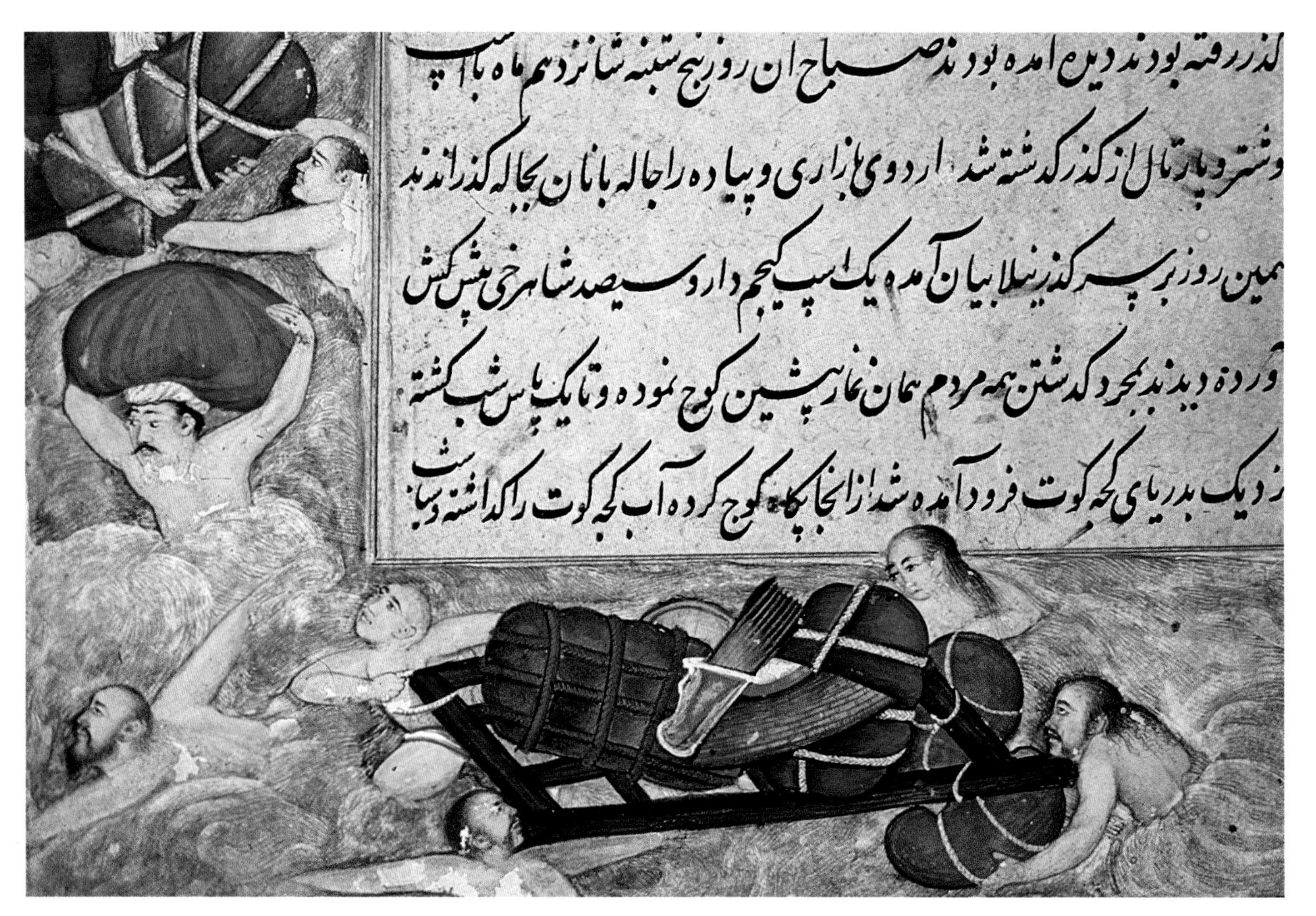
گذر رفته بودند دیر آمده بودند صباح آن روز پنجشنبه شانزدهم ماه باب
و شتر و بار تمام از گذر گذشته شد اردوی بازاری و پیاده راجاله بانان بجاله گذرانیدند
همین روز بر سر گذر نیلاب آمده یک اسپ کیچم دار و سیصد شاهرخی پیشکش
آورده دیدند بمجرد گذشتن همه مردم همان نماز پیشین کوچ نموده و تا یک پاس شب گذشته
نزدیک بدریای کچه کوت فرود آمده شد از آنجا پگاه کوچ کرده آب کچه کوت را گذاشته

گل کول
برگ کول
برگ کول
غنچه های گل کول
هاجی

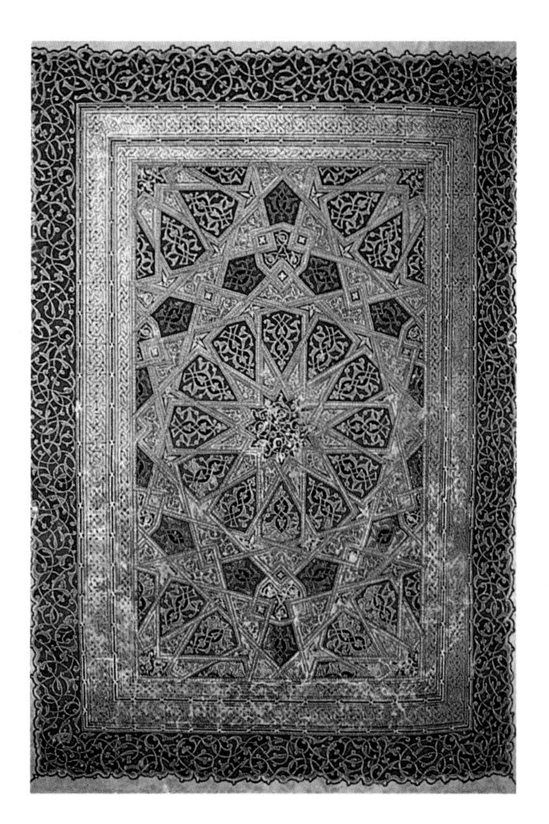

Submission to God

Gateway
Ablutions
Prayer
Koranic school
Reading the Koran
Rosary

Gateway

35 Detail from a fifteenth-century miniature representing Leyla and Majnun at school, Khamseh of Nizami. Topkapi Museum Library, Istanbul, Turkey.

36 April 1975. Bu Inaniya Medersa, fourteenth century, Fès, Morocco.

Overleaf
Frontispiece from a Koran of the Ghorid period, twelfth century. Iran Bastan Museum, Tehran, Iran.

November 1975. Decorative faience from the Attarin Medersa, fourteenth century, Fès, Morocco.

Ablutions

37 Detail from a Behzad miniature illustrating a Bustan from Saadi, fifteenth century. National Library of Cairo, Egypt.

38 September 1976. Washing fountain, Bursa, Turkey.
Before each of the five daily prayers, the Muslim must perform his ablutions.

Prayer

39 Persian miniature, sixteenth century. Malek Library, Tehran, Iran.

40 April 1975. Courtyard at the Karauin Mosque, Fès, Morocco.
When the Muslim prays, he must turn toward Mecca.

Koranic school

41 Detail from a fifteenth-century Khamseh of Nizami miniature. Topkapi Museum Library, Istanbul, Turkey.

42 March 1973. Young Turkman reading in a medersa (Koranic school) at Andkhui, Afghan Turkistan.

Reading the Koran

43 Detail from a fourteenth-century miniature. Topkapi Museum Library, Istanbul, Turkey.

44 April 1968. Tashkurgan Bazaar, Afghanistan.

Rosary

45 Fifteenth-century miniature from a Hafiz Divan, Kabul Library, Afghanistan.

46 December 1978. Prayer at Ziyaratgah, near Herat, Afghanistan.
The Muslim rosary has ninety-nine beads, symbolizing Allah's names.

39

40

Troubadours

Snow-dancer
Bear-tamer
Nasreddin Hodja
Wrestlers
Lutist
Flutist

Snow-dancer

47 December 1964. Father and son at Andar, Ghazni Province, Afghanistan. Pashtun dance, initially a war-dance. A *dhol* (drum) accompaniment is tapped out with sticks.

48 Fifteenth-century miniature, Siyah Kalem School. Topkapi Museum Library, Istanbul, Turkey.

Bear-tamer

49 Detail from a Turkish miniature from the eighteenth century. *Book of Feasts* by Vehbi. Topkapi Museum Library, Istanbul, Turkey.

50 September 1976. Region of Eskimalatya, Central Anatolia, Turkey. A Turkish proverb affirms, "If you meet a bear on a bridge, greet it softly by saying, 'my uncle,' until you have reached the other side."

Nasreddin Hodja

51 September 1964. Donkey-driver in the Bactrian Steppes, Afghanistan. Nasreddin Hodja, once master of a Koranic school and a witty sage, supposedly lived in Anatolia in the thirteenth century. His stories are a mixture of humor and folk wisdom, and are widely spread between the Mediterranean region and Central Asia.

52 Nasreddin Hodja, eighteenth century. Turkish miniature. Topkapi Museum Library, Istanbul, Turkey.

Overleaf

Miniature from a sixteenth-century album, Bukhara School. State Library, Leningrad, U.S.S.R.

March 1968. The mad sage. Mazar-i-Sharif, Afghanistan.

Wrestlers

53 Detail from a Mogul miniature, sixteenth century. National Museum of Delhi, India.

54 April 1964. Eyüp Quarter, Istanbul, Turkey.
Stripped to the waist and dressed in a stiff pair of leather shorts, both oiled from head to toe (thus the Turkish name of "oil-wrestling"), these athletes are locked in a hold.

Lutist

55 September 1976. Janissary orchestra leader, Istanbul, Turkey.

56 Detail from a Turkish miniature. *Book of Feasts* by Vehbi, eighteenth century. Topkapi Museum Library, Istanbul, Turkey.

Flutist

57 Detail from a miniature of the Tabriz School, sixteenth century. Topkapi Museum Library, Istanbul, Turkey.

58 June 1967. Dowlatabad, Meymaneh Province, Afghanistan.

47

48

53

Turkistans

Oasis
Woman in blue
Motherhood
The letter
Indian game

Oasis

59 Miniature by Siyah Kalem. *Album of the Conqueror.* Topkapi Museum Library, Istanbul, Turkey.

60 October 1976. Fall near Lake Van, Eastern Anatolia, Turkey.

Woman in blue

61 Turkish miniature by Levni, eighteenth century. Topkapi Museum Library, Istanbul, Turkey.

62 June 1967. A street in Herat, Afghanistan.
"They will have beauties with large black eyes, beauties like carefully concealed pearls."
Koran S. VI, 22.

Motherhood

63 Detail from a fifteenth-century miniature. *Album of the Conqueror.* Topkapi Museum Library, Istanbul, Turkey.

64 February 1971. Kirghiz woman feeding her child. Winter camp at Mulk Ali, Afghan Pamir.
In the Muslim Orient, women breast-feed their children for at least two years.

Overleaf
Sixteenth-century miniature taken from Matraqui's travel journal. Istanbul University Library, Turkey.

Doğubayazit Palace, Eastern Anatolia, Turkey.

The letter

65 Mogul miniature from the eighteenth century. Central Museum of Lahore, Pakistan.

66 April 1966. Young Muslim Indian from Hyderabad Province, Deccan, India.

Indian game

67 Mogul miniature from the eighteenth century. Central Museum of Lahore, Pakistan.

68 September 1966. Young Indian girls playing pachisi in the Udaipur Palace, Rajasthan, India.

59

60

Gorki "I am an Armenian from Van..."

67

68

Remembrance to God

Submission
The cloak
Man with a rose
Sage
Invocation
Shrub

Submission

69 Persian miniature, fifteenth century, school of Shiraz. Museum of Lahore, Pakistan.

70 June 1966. Muslim at Srinagar, Kashmir, India.
The word *muslim* comes from the same root as the word *islam*, which means "submission" ("he who has submitted himself to devine will").

The cloak

71 April 1968. Mahmad Niyaz in front of his shop, Tashkurgan Bazaar, Afghanistan.

72 Detail from a Siyah Kalem miniature, fifteenth century. *Album of the Conqueror.* Topkapi Museum Library, Istanbul, Turkey.

Man with a rose

73 April 1968. Mahmad Niyaz, master craftsman, Tashkurgan Bazaar, Afghanistan.

74 Portrait of Mehmet the Conqueror, fifteenth-century miniature. Topkapi Museum, Istanbul, Turkey.

Overleaf
Miniature representing Jalal ud-Din Rumi, Mevlana, founder of the dancing dervishes order. Municipal Museum, Istanbul, Turkey.

September 1976. Sheik Suleyman Hayati Dede, from the order of Mevlevi dervishes, Konya, Turkey.

Sage

75 Fifteenth-century miniature. Topkapi Museum Library, Istanbul, Turkey.

76 June 1966. Srinagar, Kashmir, India.

Invocation

77 Turkish miniature, eighteenth century. Museum of Turkish and Islamic Arts, Istanbul, Turkey.

78 August 1966. Young Muslim praying, Ajmer, Rajasthan, India.

Shrub

79 Detail from a Persian miniature. *Book of Kings,* seventeenth century. Alwar Museum, Rajasthan, India.

80 January 1972. Cappadocia, Turkey.

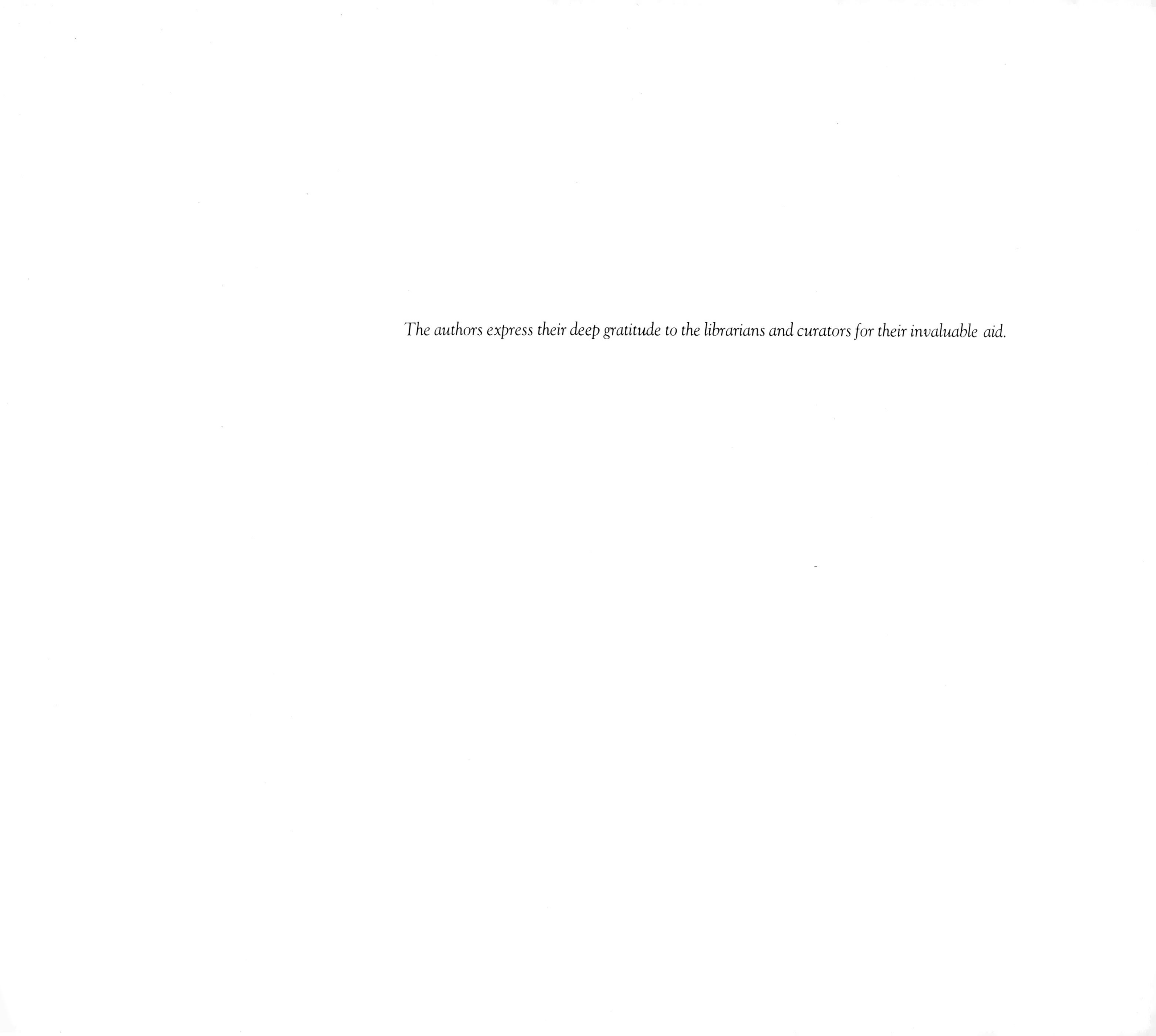

The authors express their deep gratitude to the librarians and curators for their invaluable aid.